31-DAY BIBLE STUDY FOR BLACK TEENS

Inell Williams

DAILY SCRIPTURE READINGS, AFFIRMATIONS & PROMPTS TO GROW STRONGER IN FAITH

31-DAY BIBLE STUDY FOR BLACK TEENS

____

____

TABLE OF CONTENTS

INTRODUCTION

This Bible study takes you on a 31-day journey of spiritual enrichment. It provides you a quick and convenient way to get into the habit of devoting time to God.

All verses are quoted from the World English Bible (WEB). Below the explanation of scripture, a couple of lines are provided to optionally jot down any thoughts that spring to mind. Perhaps the verse or explanation reminds you of something, or maybe you want to look up and write down another verse that is cited. Or you can jot down the meaning of a word that is new to you.

On the right-hand side of this book, each Bible verse is accompanied by an affirmation and at least two prompts to fortify your understanding, or to help you better remember the scriptures. Space is provided for brief answers.

What you'll need for this Bible study:

- a pencil or pen
- 10 minutes each day
- a heart and mind ready to connect with God

DAY 1: EQUAL UNDER GOD

GALATIANS 3:28

"There is neither Jew nor Greek, there is neither slave nor free man, there is neither male nor female; for you are all one in Christ Jesus."

In God's eyes, there are no divisions or inequalities among His children. Regardless of your background, gender, or social status, we are equally cherished, valued, and created in God's image (Genesis 1:26-28). God considers no group of people superior. Those who would say otherwise don't know that the only supreme being is Christ Himself. Take a moment to envision a diverse group of friends from different cultures, races, and economic backgrounds coming together as one tight-knit community. They celebrate each other's uniqueness and appreciate the beauty of their differences, recognizing that their worth and significance come from being part of God's family. God looks beyond the external and sees who we are at our core like no other.

My thoughts/ notes:

____

____

As a disciple of Christ, I am a descendent of Adam and a child of Abraham. No matter our background, we are all brothers and sisters in the eyes of God.

Though we are all one in God's eyes, not everyone believes this. Have you ever experienced racism, mistreatment or another form of prejudice? If yes, with a few words describe the incident.

____

____

____

Though it can be hard, we are called to forgive people who hurt us (Matthew 6:12). Write a brief prayer for the hurtful person you mentioned above. Ask God to forgive them.

____

____

____

DAY 2: FAITH & MY FUTURE

PROVERBS 16:3

"Commit your deeds to Yahweh, and your plans shall succeed."

Did you know that Yahweh - one of the many different names for God - comes from a Hebrew word that means "I am"? It means that our Lord God absolutely and simply is. This name says that He exists, has always and will always exist. We are encouraged by Him to have faith in his powerful presence. Faith in God helps us swim oceans, move mountains, fight off enemies, and leap over obstacles to reach goals in life (Matthew 17:20). It can teach us to have unwavering confidence in our plans for the future. Maintaining faith in something and persevering is a skill, so the more we do it, the better at it we will become. This is to say that whatever you strive for, whether now or in the future, just know that faith in yourself and your ability to achieve is connected to your faith in God Almighty.

My thoughts/ notes:

It doesn't matter if I'm a Black or White child of God, I can make my goals come true. God breathes life into me, and I have faith in Him. Faith helps me breathe life into my plans.

Name one specific goal that you want to accomplish in the near or distant future:

____

Imagine how would it be to have God fulfill this in your life. What would that look like? What positive results can you expect?

____

____

____

____

____

What is at least one thing you have to do to accomplish this goal?

____

DAY 3: FEAR NOT

ISAIAH 41:10

"Don't you be afraid, for I am with you. Don't be dismayed, for I am your God. I will strengthen you. Yes, I will help you. Yes, I will uphold you with the right hand of my righteousness."

Do not fear, for you are not alone. The Almighty walks by your side, strengthening and upholding you in times of distress. Just as a friend or family supports you when facing a daunting challenge, know that God stands with you, providing comfort and guidance. Imagine moving to a new town where everything feels unfamiliar and overwhelming. Instead of succumbing to fear, remember that God is there, helping you navigate through the uncertainty, making new friends, and discovering your potential in this new setting. Trust in God's presence and find courage, for He will always be with you, offering unwavering support and love during hard times. Remember that whatever fears you may feel in the present or future can be banished through Christ.

My thoughts/ notes:

____

____

Lord, when I walk through darkness and I'm afraid I might not come through the other side, I will remember that you are there shining your light at the end of the tunnel.

Is there something in your life that you fear often? Name something that made you feel fear recently.

____

____

____

Write yourself a brief prayer that you can lean on during times of distress. Keeping it short and making it rhyme can help you remember it.

____

____

____

DAY 4: YOUNG & VIRTUOUS

1 TIMOTHY 4:12

"Let no man despise your youth; but be an example to those who believe, in word, in your way of life, in love, in spirit, in faith, and in purity."

Sometimes older people can be biased against younger ones. They may forget how it was to be young, or make assumptions about you based on age. Forgive them, but don't let anyone undermine your potential because of your age. They may not always understand you nor know your heart, but the Lord does. Try and set a remarkable example for others in your speech, actions, and the way you treat others. Your influence and good character can inspire those around you to do the same, regardless of how long you've been on this Earth. Remember, your youth doesn't limit your ability to make a difference. You can be a beacon of light, like Christians are called to be (Matthew 5:14), as a testament to what young people can achieve with Christ's guidance.

My thoughts/ notes:

____

____

God shepherd me and guide me. Help me be a shining role model of the faith. I am teachable, I am receptive to the Holy Spirit, and I am yours to shape and mold.

What does being an example to those who believe look like to you?

____

____

____

What does being an example to those who believe not look like?

____

____

____

DAY 5: TEMPTATION

"No temptation has taken you except what is common to man. God is faithful, who will not allow you to be tempted above what you are able, but will with the temptation also make the way of escape, that you may be able to endure it."

You are not alone in facing temptations and challenges. Even when it feels overwhelming, remember that there is always a way out. Picture yourself in a situation where peer pressure leads you toward something you know is wrong. What could you do in that moment? You can pause and reflect. Know that God, who understands your struggles, will provide you with the strength to resist and make the right choices. Seek support from trustworthy friends, mentors, or family members who can guide you through difficult times. Trust in your own inner voice, fortified by God's wisdom, to navigate through life's trials and emerge stronger on the other side.

My thoughts/ notes:

____

____

I am human, so I am tempted. Jesus knows my flaws and loves me anyways. Praise be to Christ, my Lord and Savior.

The seven deadly sins are lust, gluttony, greed, laziness, wrath, envy, and pride. Of these, which two sins do you often find yourself most tempted by?

____

____

____

What are two specific things you can do to avoid your two common sins?

____

____

____

DAY 6: BLACK BEAUTY

"I am dark, but lovely, you daughters of Jerusalem, like Kedar's tents, like Solomon's curtains. Don't stare at me because I am dark, because the sun has scorched me..."

Back then dark skin was considered undesirable, and still is in many parts of the world. The verse here is mistranslated in most English standard versions of the Bible. It it is more likely that the speaker said "dark and lovely", since the Hebrew word used in the original text translates to "and" much more often than "but". It was assumed, though, that the woman said "dark but lovely" since a person with dark skin largely could not be considered beautiful in previous time periods. Some newer translations of the Bible recognized this mistake and use "and" instead of "but", showing that the woman in the poem is not apologizing for her dark skin; she is simply admiring her beauty.

My thoughts/ notes:

____

____

As a Black child of God, my skin - whether dark, light, or in between - is beautiful. It is a reflection of the Lord's divine creativity.

Look up the Marcia Falk translation of Song of Songs 1:5-6. Instead of "I am dark, but lovely..." what does her translation say?

____

____

____

What does God think about your skin color?

____

____

____

DAY 7: GRATITUDE

"Only fear Yahweh, and serve him in truth with all your heart; for consider what great things He has done for you."

As you go about your life, always remember to honor the Lord with sincerity and devotion. Only He can provide you with a deep feeling of fulfillment, and only He can fill you up. The bread you eat from Him is more satisfying than the bread that you can find from any other source. Even in hard or uncertain times, you can always find something to be grateful to Him for. And there are many ways that you can give the Lord thanks.

For example, try setting aside a couple of minutes for Christ in prayer each day, on both good days and bad days. You can demonstrate your gratitude by acknowledging His glory and provision day to day.

My thoughts/ notes:

____

____

Lord I thank you for all of your blessings. I am grateful. I am thank ful. Please continue to bestow blessings upon me and those I love.

Name one thing the Lord has done for you recently that you are grateful for.

____

____

____

Name at least three things that you are grateful for in your life. This could be people, things, your health, events, opportunities, etc.

____

____

____

DAY 8: CLEMENCY

PSALM 51:1-2

"Have mercy on me, God, according to your loving kindness. According to the multitude of your tender mercies, blot out my transgressions. Wash me thoroughly from my iniquity. Cleanse me from my sin."

When you are burdened with guilt or regret, turn to God. He will comfort you during these times of hardship. God is the most loving father the world has ever known. No one can match His level of mercy and care. He has the ability to forgive like no other. Open yourself to His healing grace, so that you can feel anew. Whatever you've done - whether it's a small embarrassment or a large sin - forgive yourself. Allow Him to cleanse your heart and spirit so you can move forward, restored with a sense of peace and purpose. God's clemency also teaches us how to forgive others. He has enough patience to forgive all of the people of Earth, so we can also forgive those who offend us.

My thoughts/ notes:

____

____

Forgiveness has the power to heal me. I strive to be patient with myself and others, as the Lord is patient with us all.

Sometimes bad memories or embarrassing thoughts live in our head long after their event of origin occurred. Is there something you have to forgive yourself for?

____

____

____

Do you hold a grudge against someone who trespassed against you? For your own sake, when you are ready, try to forgive them. Name the person here.

____

____

____

DAY 9: HUMILITY

1 PETER 5:5

"Likewise, you younger ones, be subject to the elder. Yes, all of you clothe yourselves with humility, to subject yourselves to one another; for 'God resists the proud, but gives grace to the humble'."

When you interact with others, approach them with humility and respect, especially those much older than you. Picture yourself in a group setting. All of your group members want to feel noticed and praised. Just like a humble coworker values the accomplishments of everyone else, you can recognize the strengths of others. Everyone has a strength of some kind, and their efforts or capabilities may be more than our own. We can humble ourselves and learn from people who are more skilled or more experienced than us. People who take on this modest mentality are often more successful than those who don't. They are wise enough to understand that they can always be better than they were yesterday by learning from others.

My thoughts/ notes:

____

____

Jesus looks out for the meek and favors the humble, so humble I shall be.

Name someone in your life who you think you can learn from. What do you admire about them?

____

____

____

Humility doesn't only apply between those who have a difference in age, as mentioned in the given verse. For what other reasons can someone be humble? Give two examples.

____

____

____

DAY 10: JUSTICE

ISAIAH 61:8

"For I, Yahweh, love justice. I hate robbery and iniquity. I will give them their reward in truth and I will make an everlasting covenant with them."

The Lord Almighty loves righteousness, and He celebrates fairness. He delights in seeing justice prevail, for that is in accordance to His goodness and holiness. Think of a real-world scenario where someone is being mistreated. It may be something you saw on the news, something that you heard from a friend, or experienced yourself. In scenarios like these, know that God stands with the mistreated, that He is advocating for them. We all know what it's like to experience anger, frustration, or hopelessness at the sight of injustice. Just know that seeking vengeance in the wrong way can spoil your righteousness (Proverbs 20:22), as it is not of God.

My thoughts/ notes:

____

____

Fairness is not always present in this world, but God has made me strong enough to handle this. In all of His glory He stands with the oppressed, and frowns upon injustice.

Can you think of something unfair in your friend group, your home, relationships, community or in current events that occupies your thoughts? It may affect you or someone else.

____

____

____

Create a brief prayer telling God about this unfairness. Acknowledge it in your prayer and then let it go, giving it to God.

____

____

____

DAY 11: WISDOM

PROVERBS 3:13-14

"Happy is the man who finds wisdom, the man who gets understanding. For her good profit is better than getting silver, and her return is better than fine gold."

Wise is the person who is a lifelong pursuer of knowledge and experience. They strive to get better at understanding themselves and the world around them so they can make better decisions. Acquiring wisdom is a process that never ends. Wise people know that you don't arrive at the gates of wisdom and exclaim, 'I've arrived!' No, for them being humble is a part of becoming wise. There is always more to learn and improve on. Strive to keep learning from your life experiences and others, especially those more experienced than you. Learn to admire people for their discipline and their depth of character, particularly those in whom you can see the hand of God.

My thoughts/ notes:

____

____

Make me more wise, o' God. I am a lifelong learner. The wisdom that you impart to me is more precious than diamonds, more valuable than gold.

What is one thing that you want to become more wise about in your life? Let God know what that is.

____

____

____

Who is someone whom you consider wise? They may be a person you know personally or not. What makes them wise?

____

____

____

DAY 12: CREATION

GENESIS 1:3-4

"God said, 'Let there be light,' and there was light. God saw the light, and saw that it was good. God divided the light from the darkness."

When the Earth was new, God banished the darkness and made everything visible with His light. In doing this, He showed that He has the power to bring illumination and clarity where there is none.

Light is a symbol of so many positive and coveted things like understanding, truth, and education. This is why God saw that light is good when He first created it. When you seek out God's wisdom and guidance, His light will illuminate your path. It will make your journey to spiritual enlightenment easier. Just like light reveals the beauty and details of a dim room, so does God's word reveal the beauty and depth of life, and of His world.

My thoughts/ notes:

____

____

I am here to be enlightened, Jesus. I want to be awash with your good light, and all of the gifts it brings.

Have you experienced being in darkness (hardship, sadness, hopelessness, lack of knowledge, etc.) and God gave you light in some way? Briefly describe it.

____

____

____

When you "see the light", that is God sharing his divine wisdom with you. When was the last time you can remember you "saw the light" in something?

____

____

____

DAY 13: WICKEDNESS

PROVERBS 6:16-19

"There are six things which Yahweh hates; yes, seven which are an abomination to him: arrogant eyes, a lying tongue, hands that shed innocent blood, a heart that devises wicked schemes..."

Some actions are simply detestable to the Lord. You may have witnessed someone engaging in low behaviors that cause chaos or hurt. These actions might include spreading false rumors or causing strife among friends. Just as toxic gossip can destroy friendships, it's important to recognize that these kinds of actions are against the values of love, kindness and peace that God wants all to uphold. So when given the choice to foster unity and build up others, or conspire in evil acts, choose the former. We're all faced with this choice sooner or later in life. Practice making a conscious effort to stand against dishonesty, cruelty and other vices, even if it means you're going against the grain. One day you'll stand at Christ's throne and your deeds will be judged.

My thoughts/ notes:

____

____

Father, I am not perfect. I have sinned before and I may sin again, but your perfection teaches me how to be better.

Name what you would consider a small act of wickedness, and name a big act of wickedness.

____

____

____

Can you think of a specific person, place, or group of people who are/ were suffering as a result of someone else's wickedness? Pray for them.

____

____

____

DAY 14: SWEET LOVE

1 CORINTHIANS 13:4-5

"Love is patient and is kind. Love doesn't envy. Love doesn't brag, is not proud, doesn't behave itself inappropriately, doesn't seek its own way, is not provoked, takes no account of evil..."

Love conquers all, as the saying goes. Let care and understanding be your guiding principle in your relationships. By embodying love's virtues, you can more easily foster deep connections. You draw people towards you when you help create a safe and warm environment where everyone feels valued and loved. When you accomplish this, people begin to associate you with God. When they feel your love, they see God's face; they feel His presence emanating through you. Love doesn't hold grudges, and isn't quick to anger. Just as a thoughtful friend listens without judgement and supports you in times of need, practice patience and understanding with those you love.

My thoughts/ notes:

____

____

Christ's love for me is endless. My love for Him is without bounds. He teaches me how to connect to people with His own selfless love.

How does God show His love in your life?

____

____

____

Name some people who you love. Ask the good Lord to watch over them.

____

____

____

DAY 15: SUPPORT

ECCLESIASTES 4:1

"If a man prevails against one who is alone, two shall withstand him; and a threefold cord is not quickly broken."

Sometimes it is easier to stand when someone stands alongside you. There are some things that we have to go through alone, but there are also times when it may well be worth it to have someone in our corner. They can give us moral support or even walk through an obstacle with us so we don't have to be alone. Jesus plays this very role for those who have no such person in their life. The world can be an unfair place, and this verse reminds us of the importance of compassion and advocacy. Instead of turning a blind eye, strive to be a voice for the voiceless, standing up against injustice and lending your support. Just as a caring friend offers comfort and assistance to those in need, extend your hand to those who are struggling. Offer others love, empathy, your time, and practical help if they want it.

My thoughts/ notes:

____

____

When I need support, I can turn to God. He uplifts me with His heavenly support, and teaches me how to stand for others.

How can you support the people around you? What about your fellow Christians?

____

____

____

Remember a time when someone lent you support in some way. Name them here, and thank them.

____

____

____

DAY 16: EVIL & SATAN

"Be sober and self-controlled. Be watchful. Your adversary, the devil, walks around like a roaring lion, seeking whom he may devour."

Imagine what would happen to you if you veered off the right path. The more you move away from that which is good, the more you become entagled with Satan and his dealings. This doesn't occur overnight. It can often start in subtle ways. Imagine what would happen if you start lying a little more. What about if you skipped school or work, or stole a small, cheap item that no one would miss? These seem minor, so they would be easy to brush off. But beware: this is how the devil starts to get a grip on you. He is constantly trying to lead all of us on the path to Hell. And Hell is not just a place where people go when they die. It can also symbolize a dark place and time that we experience on Earth as a result of our actions.

My thoughts/ notes:

____

____

Satan always lurks around the corner. Getting closer to my Lord keeps the devil at bay, in the name of Jesus!

Hell is characterized by suffering. If you experienced a personal Hell-on-Earth as a result of going down the wrong path, what might that look like for you?

____

____

____

Imagining what an earthly Hell looks like gives you something to run away from. What are you running towards instead? Name some positive things, things you would associate with Heaven.

____

____

____

DAY 17: COMPASSION

COLOSSIANS 3:12-13

"Put on therefore, as God's chosen ones, holy and beloved, a heart of compassion, kindness, lowliness, humility, and perseverance, bearing with one another, and forgiving each other..."

Having compassion means having the ability to sympathize with another person. You allow yourself to walk in their shoes and try to see the world from their perspective, especially if they're suffering or alone in some way. What if you encountered someone at church who is new, and looks uncomfortable about joining in on activities? Extend kindness by reaching out to them. You can make them feel included in the church community in small ways. Forgiveness is also a large part of compassion. Practice pardoning others when they make mistakes or hurt you unintentionally. Try to let go of grudges and offer understanding when you can. This is not only good for your heart and soul long-term, but God approves of this type of pro-compassion behavior.

My thoughts/ notes:

____

____

I am a compassionate disciple. Christ smiles on those who represent the faith with kindness and a warm heart.

When someone is very compassionate to us, it stays in our memories because it is so godly. Can you recall someone like this?

____

____

____

What are some ways you can be a compassionate disciple?

____

____

____

DAY 18: BEARING MY CROSS

LUKE 9:23

"He said to all, 'If anyone desires to come after me, let him deny himself, take up his cross [daily], and follow me'."

Following Jesus requires a daily commitment to deny yourself of harmful distractions and desires, and embrace the path that He has set for you. This will probably be uncomfortable. It may include sacrificing your personal comfort or doing things that are not popular. Just as Christ bore His own cross, in life we all have a cross to bear. Some of our crosses are more heavy than others'. And in some stages of life your cross will be heavier than in other times in your life. Either way, know that God is always with you, and will never forsake you. Lean on Him if it becomes difficult to carry. Know that He will not make you carry more than you can handle. Pray to get through rough times. He is making you stronger; it's a part of His plan.

My thoughts/ notes:

____

____

I can bear my cross just as Jesus bore His. God gives me the strength to press onward in trying times.

On a scale of 1 to 10, how strong do you think you are? Who is the strongest person that you have known in your life?

____

____

____

Say a prayer for the person you mentioned above.

____

____

____

DAY 19: SALVATION

"For by grace you have been saved through faith. And this is not your own doing; it is the gift of God, not a result of works, so that no one may boast."

You are saved through God's grace. His grace is such that He sacrificed His only son so that you may live forever. All you have to do is trust and believe in our Lord and Savior Jesus Christ in all your heart and soul. Just as you would receive a gift graciously, with appreciation, accept this salvation as a precious gift from God. Think about getting a wonderful gift from a close friend. They give it to you not because you earned it, but because they have a deep love for you. Similarly, God grants all of us His favor not because of our achievements or credentials, but because He is a kind God. He doesn't want to see humanity perish (2 Peter 3:9).

My thoughts/ notes:

____

____

Lord I call on you to save me from sin. Keep me from harm, and let me bask in your glory and become more like you each day. I accept the gift of salvation that you bestowed upon me.

How strong is your faith? If it ever wavers, how can you strengthen it?

____

____

____

As a follower of Christ, how can you give grace to others?

____

____

____

DAY 20: ANXIETY

MATTHEW 6:25

"Therefore I tell you, don't be anxious for your life: what you will eat, or what you will drink; nor yet for your body, what you will wear. Isn't life more than food, and the body more than clothing?"

If you ever find yourself feeling consumed by stress or anxiety, know that your heavenly Father is watching and cares deeply about you. Like a parent who reassures their child, God wants you to know that it is okay to feel this way, and that those feelings will pass. Let go of unnecessary worries and trust in God's provision. When you grieve about something or someone you've lost, feel anxious about your future, or you feel unconfident about your worth, remember that God is aware of your concerns and He will take care of you. Confide in Him when you are lost. Confide in Him when you lack confidence. And lean on Him when you are in need.

My thoughts/ notes:

____

____

I am bigger than the stress I feel at times. I will get through times of headache and heartache because Jesus will see me through.

What are some things you commonly feel anxious about? List them, and give them to God.

____

____

____

How can Jesus help you alleviate stress during hard times?

____

____

____

DAY 21: FRIENDSHIP

ECCLESIASTES 4:9-10

"Two are better than one, because they have a good reward for their labor. For if they fall, the one will lift up his fellow."

Good friends are truly a gift from above. They can help you overcome obstacles, and they can provide you support and encouragement during low points. Two hands toiling away together can certainly accomplish more than one. But be wary of hanging out with the wrong crowd. Your good nature can become corrupted in bad company (1 Corinthians 15:33).

It's better to be alone than with the wrong friends. If you have a friendship - in the past, present or future - that brings more joy, happiness, support or closeness in your life, cherish it, especially if it is of God. If you no longer have a friend like that, but you did, cherish the memory of your friendship. Embrace the strength that comes from having a Godly companion in life.

My thoughts/ notes:

Glory be to Him who sends me a true and good friend. As one of the most treasured gifts my God can give me, I am grateful for them.

What does a godly friend look like?

____

____

____

Do you see God's face in your close circle?

____

____

____

DAY 22: SPIRITUAL WARFARE

EPHESIANS 6:12

"For our wrestling is not against flesh and blood, but against the principalities, against the powers, against the world's rulers of the darkness of this age, and against the spiritual forces of wickedness in the heavenly places."

Your struggles are not only against opponents that you can see, but also against spiritual forces of darkness. Though their influence is sometimes not clear, it is certainly felt. Picture a scenario where you are faced with pressures and temptations that seem overwhelming. It's like being in the world of a video game. Enemies and obstacles are put in your path to hinder your progress in the game, and you have to fight through them. Like this, there are spiritual battles occurring all around you, though they may not be in plain view. It's important to be aware of harmful influences and distracting ideologies that threaten to push you further away from Christ and lead you closer to Lucifer.

My thoughts/ notes:

____

____

As a disciple, I accept that spiritual warfare is a right of passage. It is a part of my plight and purpose as a Christian.

The good fight for faith looks different for every generation of Christians. What ideas or forms of groupthink may threaten to take you off a godly path today?

____

____

____

How can you strengthen yourself against ideas that go against God?

____

____

____

DAY 23: I AM A SINNER

MARK 2:17

"When Jesus heard it, he said to them, "Those who are healthy have no need for a physician, but those who are sick. I came not to call the righteous, but sinners to repentance."

No one on Earth can say that they have never sinned. We've all fallen short of the glory of Christ in one way or another, and will continue to do so. As such, Jesus knows that we are all flawed and can use His guidance to be better than we were yesterday. Acknowledging that you're flawed and that it's okay can give you the courage to strive to become more Christ-like.

God doesn't seek perfection nor a show of righteousness from you. He values your honest, humble self-assessment. It's okay if someone can be self aware enough to realize that they are not without fault, or may have made wrong choices. God still welcomes you with open arms.

My thoughts/ notes:

____

____

When I have fallen short, when I have disappointed, and when I have been less than good, God is still my friend.

God calls all sinners to repentance. Do you have something that you want to repent on?

____

____

____

We can repent through words and prayer, which God favors. But how does repentance also look like through actions?

____

____

____

DAY 24: GOD IS SOVEREIGN

"Yours, Yahweh, is the greatness, the power, the glory, the victory, and the majesty! For all that is in the heavens and in the earth is yours. Yours is the kingdom, Yahweh, and you are exalted as head above all."

The word sovereign means that something has absolute power or is supreme. To understand just how profound God's greatness is, imagine standing on a mountaintop and looking down at the vastness of nature and all of the beauty of creation. As this view overwhelms your senses, realize that everything in your field of vision, and everything in Heaven and on Earth belong to Him. Everything you have and all that surrounds you comes from God. That's why He is known as the Lord Almighty. Your possessions, your talents, your memories and loved ones, everything is a gift from Him to you. Even the breath from your lungs would not exist without God. His ownership extends over all things.

My thoughts/ notes:

____

____

There is no higher god but God. He reigns supreme. He sits on high. He looks downward towards me, His creation, with a love and grace like no other!

How great is our God? Take a few sentences to worship and give glory to Him.

____

____

____

Remember that we are created in God's image (Genesis 1:26-28). What does this say about how God views us as human beings?

____

____

____

DAY 25: ETERNAL LIFE

JOHN 6:50-51

"This is the bread which comes down out of heaven, that anyone may eat of it and not die. I am the living bread which came down out of heaven. If anyone eats of this bread, he will live forever."

Jesus Christ offers a deep sense of purpose, fulfillment, and eternal hope to all of the hungry souls who seek Him out. Just like you turn to a nourishing meal to satisfying your bodily hunger, Christ offers Himself as the bread that will satisfy your spiritual hunger. He provides sustenance that goes beyond our worldly abode. Have you ever experienced a time when you felt spiritually depleted, searching in vain to satisfy your deepest longings? Only God can fill that gaping hole. So embrace His invitation to eat with Him at His heavenly table, and feast on His teachings to find true satisfaction that extends far beyond temporary pleasures.

My thoughts/ notes:

____

____

Christ's bread of Heaven is enough to satisfy me. With it I have everything, and I want for nothing.

Make a list of some temporary pleasures that you like to indulge in.

____

____

____

Look at the list above that you created. List the positive feelings that these pleasures give you.

____

____

____

Know that all of positives you listed are what you can find through God's counsel, but in greater depth!

DAY 26: LONELINESS

"...Don't abandon me, neither forsake me, God of my salvation. When my father and my mother forsake me, then Yahweh will take me up."

Just as a loving parent rushes to find and comfort their child, God is there for you in your times of distress. He never abandons you. When you feel overwhelmed or alone, He's there. When you feel that you have to face fear and uncertainty alone, know that He is with you. Seek His guidance and cherish His presence, for it is like a strong and reliable shelter that can offer you safety and reassurance. Even if you come to a time in your life where you have no one to call family, no one to call a friend, trust that Jesus can fill those roles for you. Wherever you are now in your life, your home is with Him. He walks beside you even if you can't see Him. In dark times, you can look above and see Jesus' light shining through to comfort you.

My thoughts/ notes:

____

____

Even if earthly beings leave me by myself and lonesome, God above does not forsake me.

We all have different ways of getting closer to God especially when we are lonely. What are some ways you feel most connected to God?

____

____

____

Why do you think God doesn't forsake you?

____

____

____

DAY 27: KEEP THE FAITH

2 TIMOTHY 3:14-15

"But you remain in the things which you have learned and have been assured of... From infancy, you have known the holy Scriptures which are able to make you wise for salvation through faith, which is in Christ Jesus."

Like a compass that points you in the right direction, allow the Bible to shape your beliefs, values, and life decisions. The Scriptures provide you with a firm foundation to stand upon, and helps bolster your faith. Studying scriptures alone can be difficult though. It could be helpful for you to have a wise mentor or teacher who imparts knowledge and guidance to you if you don't have one already. Or to join or form a study group with like-minded people. This kind of group can give everyone gentle encouragement to continue studying The Good Book, and internalize all of its wisdom. In your spiritual journey, remember to ground yourself in the teachings and wisdom passed on to you.

My thoughts/ notes:

____

____

I am steadfast in my faith. I am a dutiful disciple. I am loyal to my God, and I want to know how to better serve Him each day.

A lot of us struggle with faith sometimes. When do you find yourself struggling with faith?

____

____

____

Some invest more time into their faith by creating faith-based music playlists, teaching a younger family member scriptures, joining mission trips, creating a prayer schedule, etc. Besides doing this Bible study, what do you like to do? Or what would you like to do in the future to invest more time towards God?

____

____

____

DAY 28: FAMILY

1 TIMOTHY 5:8

"But if anyone doesn't provide for his own, and especially his own household, he has denied the faith, and is worse than an unbeliever."

One of the greatest responsibilities God gave you in this life is to care for your family and loved ones. You are called to provide for and support your family. How this provision looks varies depending on what your role is among your kin. It doesn't only mean finances, though that is one important way to provide, especially for men. It can also mean providing support and care, and being present in their lives. A well-functioning team relies on each member to do their part. Your family can flourish when everyone makes a pact to take care of one another. Some family members are understandably difficult to lend support to though. The path they choose may not be of God. In circumstances such as these, even if they're blood, it is wise to keep a loving distance, lest they stray you away from that which is good.

My thoughts/ notes:

____

____

My family, whatever form it may take, is important to me. I am dutiful to my kin, just as God calls me to be.

How do you care for your family members? Under what circumstances might you not support a family member, if any?

____

____

____

Who is worse than a nonbeliever?

____

____

____

DAY 29: WORK & PERSEVERANCE

PROVERBS 18:9

"One who is slack in his work is brother to him who is a master of destruction."

Sloth and neglect can wreak havoc in your life if you're not careful. God knows that everyone struggles with procrastination and laziness at one point or another - some of us more than others - but it's important to be mindful of the dangers of laziness and neglecting important tasks. Ignoring responsibilities leads to incomplete or subpar results, and laziness can hinder your overall progress with your life goals. If these become long-term habits, you can prevent yourself from reaching your full potential. That is why slackness is compared to destruction in this verse: by being slack today, you might destroy your potential tomorrow. But if you actively take charge of your commitments and invest effort into them, you open doors to new opportunities and achieve meaningful outcomes. So try to avoid having a habit of slothing and slacking off, and God will reward you for your efforts.

My thoughts/ notes:

____

____

With God's help I am capable of pushing myself to work harder and smarter over time. In doing this I am securing my future and taking care of my future self.

Using any Bible translation you'd like, look up 2 Thessalonians 3:10. What does it say?

____

____

____

Do you have anything that you want to procrastinate less? Or some responsibilities you may have avoided? If so, what are they?

____

____

____

DAY 30: THE POWER OF PRAYER

COLOSSIANS 4:2

"Continue steadfastly in prayer, watching in it with thanksgiving..."

Make prayer a priority in your life. Setting aside moments to converse with God can do a whole lot of good for you, for your future, and for your mental health. Bear in mind that whatever you pray for, you are more likely to receive (Mark 11:24). A lot of us have a close friend or special someone with whom we connect deeply, whom we enjoy spending time with. Maybe you have one. You eagerly make time for this person. You share your thoughts with them and listen to what they have to say. Similarly, God desires a deep and personal relationship with you. You can achieve this relationship with Him through prayer. Prayer gives you the opportunity to express your joys, concerns, and gratitude to Jesus. As this verse prescribes, keep watch of your past prayers. For the ones that God does answer, in accordance with His plan, always give thanks.

My thoughts/ notes:

____

____

I will pray and pray for others and for myself. Prayer cleanses my soul and keeps me grounded as a Christian.

Look up the verse Matthew 6:5-6. What does it say?

____

____

____

What are some prayers that Jesus has answered for you? Take a few moments to thank Him for them.

____

____

____

DAY 31: RESURRECTION

"For if we believe that Jesus died and rose again, even so God will bring with him those who have fallen asleep in Jesus."

The Lord tells us that if you believe in His resurrection with all of your heart and soul, you will be saved (Romans 10:9). Resurrection extends to humanity as well. As death was not the final chapter in Jesus's story, it also is not the final chapter in our spiritual lives. If you have faith in Jesus, you will rise again like Him. For those who have past and left you, find comfort in the hope of eternal reunion with them again in the afterlife. If you choose to believe in the Gospel, death is not the end. This separation from your loved one(s) will only last for a short time, though it may seem long to you. To Elohim human life is short, and time is vast and unending. The Lord is watching over you, and He knows your pain. Take this into consideration the next time you or someone you know fear death or grieve for someone who has passed on.

My thoughts/ notes:

____

____

I am awed by the idea of eternal life with God in His heavenly kingdom. I thank Him for sacrificing His son so that I may have a deathless death.

Do you have someone whom you miss? Say a prayer for them and for yourself.

____

____

____

What do you think Heaven looks like? Who would you look forward to seeing there?

____

____

____

If you're a gal, check out
15-Minute Bible Workbook or
Healing Affirmations:

If you're a guy, check out
35-Day Bible Study:

www.ingramcontent.com/pod-product-compliance
Lightning Source LLC
Chambersburg PA
CBHW051008050726
47592CB00007B/2764